W9-COG-239

WITHDRAWN

Donated to
SAINT PAUL PUBLIC LIBRARY

WITHDRAWN

Crabapples

Kids perform CIRCUS Arts

Bobbie Kalman

 Crabtree Publishing Company

Crabapples

created by Bobbie Kalman

For Samantha
in memory of happy times

Editor-in-Chief
Bobbie Kalman

Writing team
Bobbie Kalman
Petrina Gentile

Managing editor
Lynda Hale

Editors
Petrina Gentile
Niki Walker

Consultants
Carrie Heller, Circus Arts Inc.;
Elsie Smith, San Francisco
School of Circus Arts

Computer design
Lucy DeFazio
Lynda Hale

Color separations and film
Dot 'n Line Image Inc.

Special thanks to
Carrie Heller; Elsie Smith; Dan Gould, Nigel Watson, Jackie Tan,
Blas Viera, and the circus performers at Independent Lake Camp;
Samantha Crabtree; Club Med; Jillian Feldman; Darwin Hamilton;
Ileana Guanchez; Erika Bergen; Anna Hirst; Anatoly Butko and the
students of the National Circus School of Canada, including
Nicole Canejo, Anton Nikoulina, and Nathan Fraser; Carol Harder
and the students of Virgil Public School; and Maria Simone

Photographs
Chris Conrad Corry: pages 26 (both), 29
Marc Crabtree: pages 8 (left), 9, 11, 13
Greg Furminger/Niagara Falls Review: page 7 (top)
Bobbie Kalman and Peter Crabtree: cover, back cover, title page,
    pages 6 (all), 7 (bottom), 8 (right), 10 (top), 12 (bottom),
    14, 15 (right), 17, 18 (both), 19 (both), 20 (both), 21 (both),
    22 (top), 25 (both), 28
David Sands: pages 4, 5, 10 (bottom left and right), 12 (top),
    15 (left), 16, 22 (bottom), 23 (all), 24, 30 (both), 31

Printer
Worzalla Publishing Company

Crabtree Publishing Company

350 Fifth Avenue
Suite 3308
New York
N.Y. 10118

360 York Road, RR 4,
Niagara-on-the-Lake,
Ontario, Canada
L0S 1J0

73 Lime Walk
Headington
Oxford OX3 7AD
United Kingdom

Copyright © **1997 CRABTREE PUBLISHING COMPANY**.
All rights reserved. No part of this publication may be
reproduced, stored in a retrieval system or be transmitted
in any form or by any means, electronic, mechanical,
photocopying, recording, or otherwise, without the prior
written permission of Crabtree Publishing Company.

Cataloging in Publication Data
Kalman, Bobbie
    Kids perform circus arts

(Crabapples)
Includes index.

ISBN 0-86505-630-7 (library bound)   ISBN 0-86505-730-3 (pbk.)
This book shows children learning and performing circus arts
such as juggling, the Spanish Web, and the trapeze.

1. Acrobatics - Juvenile literature. 2. Circus - Juvenile
literature. I. Title. II. Series: Kalman, Bobbie. Crabapples.

GV552.K35 1996   j796.47   LC 96-35196
                                         CIP

What is in this book?

What is a circus?

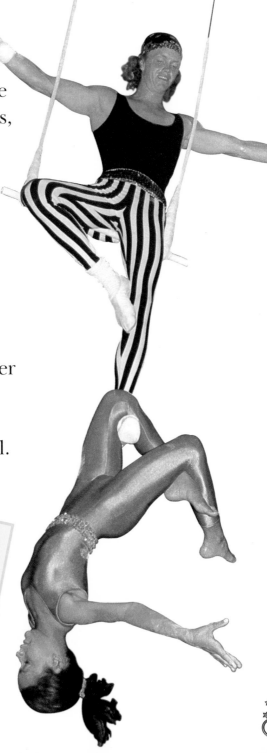

A circus is a magical show with acrobats, clowns, jugglers, cyclists, and trapeze artists. Some circuses use real animals, but this book has only pretend ones.

Performing circus arts is daring and fun. Can you imagine the thrill of juggling on a unicycle, flying high on a trapeze, or balancing on top of a human pyramid?

These acts may seem hard to do, but you can learn them with a good teacher and lots of practice. Being a circus performer will make you feel special because it is challenging and unusual.

Performing circus arts will...
- give you confidence
- make you more creative
- help you deal with your fears
- increase your concentration
- make your body stronger and more flexible
- improve your balance
- teach you to work as part of a team

Clowning around

Clowns are a fun part of the circus. There are three types—**white-face**, **auguste**, and **character**. A white-face clown has a white face and neck. Auguste clowns wear colorful, silly costumes. Character clowns wear everyday clothes. You can create a combination of all three.

Most clowns do not talk. They use gestures and facial expressions to communicate. This type of clowning is called **pantomiming** or **miming**.

Clowns will do anything to make people laugh. They play tricks and act silly. They might even hang upside-down to get a chuckle!

Juggling tricks

Juggling takes concentration, patience, and lots of practice! Most people learn to juggle by throwing three scarves in the air. The scarves fall slowly, making them easy to catch.

Juggling balls, pins, or rings is much harder than juggling scarves. Juggling while riding on a unicycle is even harder! It takes a lot of skill and concentration. Be careful—don't look down!

There are many ways to juggle, but most people use a **cascade** or **shower** pattern. Using a cascade pattern, a juggler crisscrosses the objects in the air. The juggler on the opposite page is juggling the balls in a circular, or shower, pattern.

Acrobats and contortionists

Acrobats jump, flip, and somersault across the floor. They balance, leap, and swoop while walking on tightropes. They flip and fly through the air on a trapeze. Acrobats include cyclists, balancers, and trapeze artists.

Can you put your legs behind your head or touch your ears with your toes? **Contortionists** can! They are so flexible that they can bend their body into positions that seem impossible!

Balancing acts

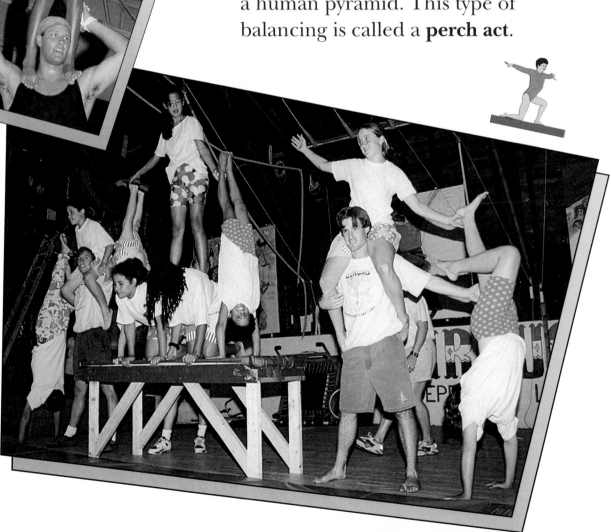

In a circus, balancing is part of many acts. Acrobats use poles, umbrellas, and their arms to keep their balance.

The performers below are building a human pyramid. This type of balancing is called a **perch act**.

Find the different ways acrobats are using balance in this book. Think of five ways you use balance every day.

Cycling stunts

Imagine trying to ride a unicycle or bicycle with a group of people. It is a balancing act that requires teamwork. If one person makes a wrong move, the whole group could take a tumble!

Each rider shown here is balancing four children as he rides around in circles. The group below is performing a trick called the **tulip**. The girl on the rider's shoulders leans back to make the top of the tulip. Another child sits on the handlebar facing the rider. He is the tulip's bottom. He holds the girl's ankles as she bends backwards. Two **sides** help the rider balance. They raise their arms to form the tulip's petals.

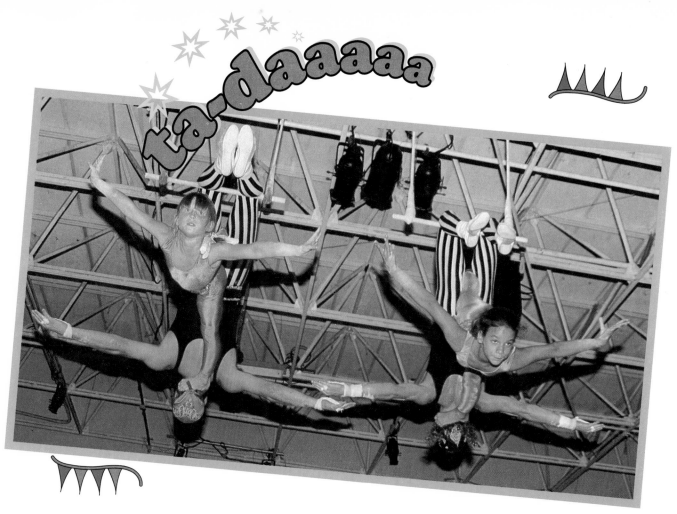

ta-daaaaa

On the trapeze

There are several kinds of trapeze acts. In the **double trapeze**, two acrobats perform together on a bar that hangs from the ceiling by two ropes. The bar does not swing during the act. Sometimes it is 20 feet (7 meters) above the floor! There is a thick mat under the trapeze and one or two adults to help. The act shown above is a **side-by-side** double. There are two acrobats on each swing. To reach the trapeze, the smaller acrobats climb the bigger ones as if they were ladders. Then they hang only by an ankle and a foot.

The **triple trapeze** is a bar that is wide enough for three. These six acrobats are performing a move called the **bird's nest**.

The swinging trapeze

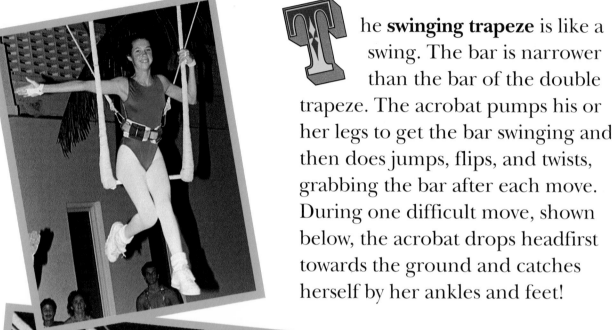

The **swinging trapeze** is like a swing. The bar is narrower than the bar of the double trapeze. The acrobat pumps his or her legs to get the bar swinging and then does jumps, flips, and twists, grabbing the bar after each move. During one difficult move, shown below, the acrobat drops headfirst towards the ground and catches herself by her ankles and feet!

The flying trapeze

The **flying trapeze** is performed high above a large net. The acrobats, called **flyers**, climb up a narrow ladder. It can be scary to look down! They step onto a small platform and grab the bar. They swing over the net, performing moves. Sometimes they are caught by an acrobat on the next trapeze bar. This person is the **catcher**. Catchers must be strong in order to grab and hold the flyers coming towards them.

Samantha is about to grab the bar and swing off the platform towards the catcher. She uses a **knee-hang** position, shown below. When the catcher is ready to grab her, he calls "*listo*," which means "ready" in Spanish. The catcher grabs Samantha's wrists and she straightens her legs, as shown at the top of the opposite page.

Samantha lets go of her bar, and she and the catcher swing together. When it is time for Samantha to grab her bar again, he calls "hep." She must now make a tricky move called a **return**. She has to turn around in mid-air and grab the swing she left. If she misses, the bar will swing away without her, and she will land on the safety net below. The **splits** position, shown right, is another trick performed on the flying trapeze.

Spanish Web

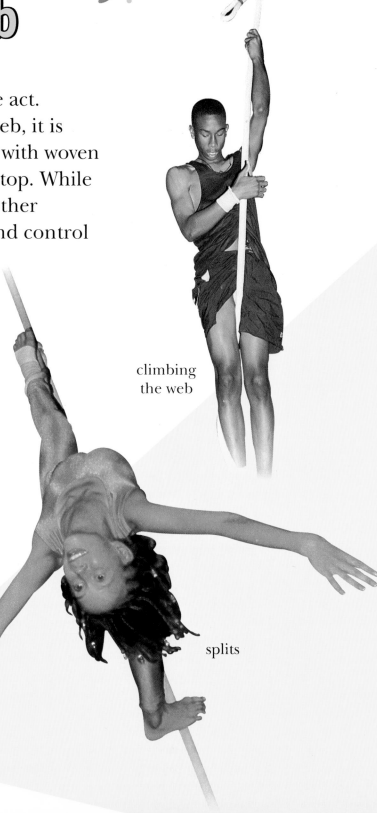

The Spanish Web is a rope act. Although it is called a web, it is actually a rope covered with woven fabric that has a loop near the top. While one person is on the web, another person stands below to spin and control the rope. This person is called the **web-setter**.

An acrobat must have strong arms and legs to climb up the web. With practice, some acrobats can climb the web using only their arms!

The acrobat places a hand or foot through the loop. It has a safety device called a **keeper** that slides up and down. Acrobats move the keeper to tighten the loop around their wrist or ankle. The loop keeps them in place as they hang and spin.

climbing the web

splits

flag-out, figure 4, or preparation for a handspin

back arch

splits or layback

The most exciting part of a Spanish Web routine is the spin. The girl in the picture above is preparing to be spun by the web-setter. Soon she will be just a blur to the audience, who will gasp, cheer, whistle, and clap—a lot!

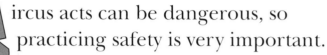

Playing it safe

ircus acts can be dangerous, so practicing safety is very important. Warming up before a routine helps prevent injuries and improve flexibility. Walking, stretching, and doing situps and pushups helps warm, or **limber up**, the muscles. Cooling down afterwards is also important.

Drinking plenty of water and breathing properly help your muscles perform their best. If your body is shaky, you need to rest and drink more water.

Acrobats practice a move over and over again. They always work with a **spotter**. A spotter is an adult who is trained in teaching circus arts. He or she checks the equipment to make sure it is safe to use. The spotter then stands nearby to help the acrobats or catch them if they fall.

The acrobat on page 24 is wearing a **safety harness**. If she slips from the trapeze, the harness will slow her fall. On the ground, a thick foam mat ensures a soft landing.

A safety net keeps flying trapeze performers from being injured. The acrobats are taught how to fall properly onto the net. They land flat on their back in the middle of the net. They avoid the edge of the net so they will not bounce off. When it is time to **dismount**, a spotter helps the acrobats somersault off the net.

Before beginning some trapeze and Spanish Web acts, acrobats cover their hands, wrists, and ankles with chalk. Chalk helps prevent slipping by keeping the skin dry. Some acrobats also wear gloves during a routine. Others wrap their wrists in cloth to avoid slipping off the rope or bar.

Put on a show!

You can plan, or **frame**, your own circus show—with the help of adults, of course! Most shows last 90 minutes and have 12 acts. Think of the acts you want to have—**zanies**, **pongers**, and lots of other **kinkers**. Hand out **heralds** to attract the **flatties**, and you're sure to have a **turnaway**!

Don't forget! You will also need spotters, **spielers**, **shanties**, or **chandeliers**, and **windjammers**.

If the words we used make no sense to you, find them on the opposite page. Have lots of fun preparing for your show!

Circus talk

Here are some common circus words and phrases. Use them to talk about your circus show.

"All out and over"—the show is finished

chandelier—the person in charge of lights

clown walk-around—a parade of clowns that perform their acts as they walk

"Doors!"—It is time to let in the audience!

first of May—a first-time performer in a circus show

flatties—spectators

flyer—a flying-trapeze artist

frame a show—plan a show

herald—circus announcement or advertisement

Joey—a clown; short for Joseph Grimaldi, a famous British clown

kinker—originally meant acrobat; now refers to all circus performers

on the show—everyone involved with the circus

ponger—an acrobat

shanty—*see* chandelier

spieler—the person who introduces the circus acts

turnaway—a sold-out show

windjammer—a person in a circus band

zanies—clowns

Showtime!

Putting on a circus show takes lots of practice and planning. You have rehearsed your routines over and over, and you feel confident and excited. The moment has come to show off all your hard work. It's showtime!

There is more
to a circus than
exciting acts.
Colorful masks,
wigs, and hats
are all part of
a dazzling show.
You can use
costumes and
makeup to give
yourself a beautiful,
funny, or silly appearance.

Circus schools and camps

o you want to join the circus? You can learn circus arts at vacation resorts and summer camps. In the past few years, circus arts have become so popular that they are being offered at many locations. There are big circus schools in some cities, but smaller schools are opening all over the country.

Some gymnastic schools are making circus arts a part of their program. Many elementary schools are also teaching circus arts. Find a program in your area and start right away. You will love it!

CIRCUS SCHOOL
ECOLE DU CIRQUE

Words to know

acrobat A person who is skilled in performing moves, such as swinging on a trapeze

catcher The person who catches acrobats on the flying trapeze

circus arts The study and performance of circus acts such as the Spanish Web

contortionist A person who can bend his or her body into many positions

cyclist A person who rides a bicycle

dismount A move an acrobat makes to get off a piece of equipment

keeper The safety device attached to a loop on the Spanish Web

limber up To stretch or warm up muscles before performing an act

routine A set of moves in a circus act

safety harness A safety device that slows down an acrobat's fall

side An acrobat who rides on the side of a bicycle during a bicycle routine

somersault A tumble or roll in which a person's body turns a complete circle

spotter An adult who teaches and assists acrobats with their routine

trapeze A short bar that hangs from two ropes

unicycle A one-wheeled vehicle with pedals

trick Any move in a circus routine

web-setter The person who spins the rope in the Spanish Web act

Index

32

1 2 3 4 5 6 7 8 9 0 Printed in USA 6 5 4 3 2 1 0 9 8 7